T0208215

Marking
Time with
Mark

A Devotional Journal
on the Book of Mark

JANET FISHER ARONSON

WESTBOW
PRESS®
A DIVISION OF THOMAS NELSON
& ZONDERVAN

WestBow Press books may be ordered through booksellers or by contacting:

WestBow Press
A Division of Thomas Nelson & Zondervan
1663 Liberty Drive
Bloomington, IN 47403
www.westbowpress.com
1 (866) 928-1240

ISBN: 978-1-9736-5922-8 (sc)
ISBN: 978-1-9736-5921-1 (e)

Print information available on the last page.

WestBow Press rev. date: 4/19/2019

This book is dedicated to my Spiritual Moms

Carol Lohnes

Marianne Lundberg

Gail Berry

Without their encouragement, I would
not be the woman I am today.

Acknowledgements

First and foremost, I thank the Lord for the incredible privilege of serving him, for giving me the gift of words and for always being with me as I wrote.

There are so many people who have helped to make this book possible. Those who have gone before me, who encouraged me to be all that I could be in Christ. I will never be able to express my gratitude.

Thanks to my readers on *Stepping Up*. Your faithfulness and encouragement made it worth getting up every morning to write.

To my friends and family. Also, my faithful Bible study group. Thanks for your support and love.

Thanks to Denis Keith, my coach, mentor and friend. Thank you for helping me through some tough stuff and encouraging me to start anew. Thanks also for reading the book and offering your input.

Thanks also to my pastor, Bob Sheldon for taking the time to review and offer insight on the book.

Thanks to my sister, Ellen Fisher Smith, for doing the tough job of editing the manuscript and catching all my grammatical errors.

Introduction

Mark had a mission. He wanted the good news to spread and the story to be told. I relate to Mark because, like him, I tend to just give the facts when I write. Mark's style is concise and yet it connects the message to the prophecies about the Messiah.

A few years ago, I felt called to share my musings on various things I read in Scripture in an on-line setting. I invited a few friends to join me to take a pause in their day to ponder God's word and his message. This devotional was one of the studies we did. The group on Facebook is called *Stepping Up: Growing Up in Christ Together.* The idea was that we would read, reflect on and respond to a passage in Scripture.

With that in mind, I encourage you to do the same. First, read the Scripture. Take time with it, write your own notes. Second, read the devotional. Each one contains questions, thoughts and information. Reflect on what you've read. Finally, take time to respond in the space for journaling. Answer one of the questions, react to a statement, or just let your thoughts flow to what God is saying to you.

Finally, use these devotionals as opportunities to share the message of the Gospel with those you know.

To God be the Glory,
Janet

The Journey Begins

A Voice in the Wilderness
Mark 1:1-13

Because we have the other gospels, we know the back story of Jesus birth from Luke, his genealogy, his visit to the temple (Luke 2). Here in Mark it seems that he came out of nowhere. And this is true. With the exception of that visit to Jerusalem at the age of 12, there is no record of him doing or saying anything until his 30th year. He lived his life with family in Nazareth. It makes you wonder what went on during those years.

And John suddenly appears on the horizon, calling for repentance and baptism. Into a world that was struggling with war and occupation, John's ministry was to call for a reform of the heart, to draw people to God so that they would recognize Messiah.

I think a lot about John. He knew his mission and his part in the bigger story. He knew what he was supposed to do and how he was supposed to live. It's interesting that Mark, being so concise about what he says, includes what John was wearing and eating. It showed him as a man of the desert but also as a prophet, like Elijah, who came to declare the coming of the Lord. John stood out to the people because of this.

Mark uses the passage from Isaiah to begin his account. "I will send my messenger ahead of you, who will prepare your way"-- "a voice of one calling in the desert, 'Prepare the way for the Lord, make straight paths for him.'" (Isaiah 40:3) In other translations, we find the word "highway" or "pathway" used, and Mark is all about the path to Christ, the path to God. We will see the words "way" and "path" used many times in the book. The message is that we are on a journey to God, following the pathway that he has given us through his Son. John's message was clear: "I am here to announce the coming of Messiah. I am not the One."

And then, Jesus came. God proclaimed him to be the Son, the one John had announced. Imagine being one of the people who had come out to hear John. It doesn't say that they heard the voice, but something must have happened. The Holy Spirit had come down, things were changing. John knew it, so did Jesus.

And then nothing for 40 days. Did John wonder where Jesus went? Did he wonder if he was mistaken? He certainly asks the question later. "Are you the One?" (Matthew 11:2).

As we look at this brief synopsis of the beginning of Jesus ministry, what stands out to you? For me it is how little we really know about him, and how God orchestrated the whole thing. John's clear message – HE'S COMING! BE PREPARED!

Are you prepared for him in your life? Have you taken steps to confess and be forgiven, to open yourself to whatever He calls you to do? John was. I want to be too.

Journal your thoughts:

_____

_____

_____

_____

_____

_____

_____

_____

_____

_____

_____

_____

_____

_____

_____

_____

_____

_____

Ordinary People
Mark 1:14-28

I love the way Mark jumps right into the good news. No flowery talk, no hesitation. Here is Jesus. Here is the good news. Believe it!

I also love that Jesus had a plan: preach the good news, gather the disciples, cast out the darkness. Wow, all in 15 verses!

But what I love most is how he chose those disciples because it says something to each of us. There they were sitting on the beach, fishing and fixing their nets. Two sets of brothers. As it says in Acts 4:13, they were simple, uneducated men, uncomplicated, but open to the good news. What does this say to you? Have you struggled with feeling "less than"? God made you who you are and placed you where you are for a purpose. Do you wonder if you can be of any use, because you are just a _____? (fill in the blank). God uses simple, ordinary people to take his good news to the world, their world.

I love those four men who dropped everything to go with Jesus. And they remained with him, learning and growing and becoming the men God used to change the world. How about you? Do you remain with Jesus, learning and growing? Maybe it's time to step out and change your little corner of the world for the Kingdom.

It didn't take a lot of time for the word to spread. Jesus had an authority that was not seen in the teachers of the law and it showed. He cast out the demons with authority. He spoke from the Scriptures with authority. He showed right up front that he was different. The word spread.

Looking forward to the book of Acts, we see that the authority of Jesus was passed on to his disciples so that the good news went from a little corner of the world to the whole known world in only a few decades. And the world was changed by those simple men who walked away from their fishing nets into something beyond their imagination. They were set on fire by a simple invitation to "Come, follow Me."

Imagine yourself taking a step of faith in order to fulfill God's plan through you to the world. Are you ready to take that step? Is he calling you out of your comfort zone to a task beyond what you can imagine? Get up and get going! The time is now! The Kingdom is near! The Lord has come and is coming again! Maranatha! Come, Lord Jesus!

Journal your thoughts:

_____

_____

_____

_____

_____

_____

_____

_____

_____

_____

_____

_____

_____

_____

Start with Prayer
Mark 1:29-45

"Very early in the morning, while it was still dark..." Mark mentions this three times in his gospel. Jesus rose early to pray. He did this when he needed to take a break and meet with his Father. He did this for a purpose. And he did this for strength in the midst of stressful times.

As Jesus left the synagogue, he knew that people would see and want miracles. He knew that while this was important to his mission, it was not the point. He knew that, in order to keep the focus on the "good news", he would have to keep focused himself. Prayer was the answer.

If Jesus needed to connect with God the Father, we must need that too. Maybe your prayer life has gotten dry or even non-existent. Take the time right now to commit to praying for the things that God has put on your heart. Jesus did.

The people came for healing and miracles, but what they needed was salvation and renewed relationship with God. Jesus knew this and worked to keep the balance between the spectacular and the essential. His ministry could have become all about performing miracles, but as we read earlier in the chapter, he truly wanted to meet with the people in the synagogues and bring forth the Word of God. He wanted to bring revival to the Jews, to God's people. He wanted them to open their hearts to God's love and forgiveness.

So why didn't the leper do as he was told? Why did he spread the word about Jesus' healing miracles? And why doesn't God do things our way? Why do people mess it up?

These are all good questions. They hint at a bigger and better way. God uses people to complete his purposes. Sometimes they listen to directions and sometimes they don't, but in all of it God's purposes are fulfilled. So, while Jesus wanted to meet the people in the synagogues, he had to use a different plan, a broader plan. He had to be on the move, drawing the crowds to the out of the way places where he could share the good news.

Have you ever had your plans disrupted by well-meaning people? What should you do? Jesus got to work, praying and preaching wherever God sent him. Don't get discouraged, don't give up. Take the opportunity to expand your view of what you are to do. And pray and serve as God reveals his purposes to you.

Journal your thoughts:

_____

_____

_____

_____

_____

_____

_____

_____

_____

_____

_____

_____

_____

_____

_____

_____

_____

Faith-Filled
Mark 2:1-17

Faith. So difficult to define and explain to those who don't have it. Faith can move mountains, carry us through the valley of death, heal our fears and keep us on track. Faith is the belief that what is unseen is still real. Faith tells us to take a risk, to speak a word, to live out the fruit of the Spirit. We are called to live by faith.

As Jesus resumed his ministry, the crowds grew larger and larger. They surrounded the home where he was staying. They came in droves to hear him teach the word, the message of the Kingdom. Into that teaching moment one group of friends saw an opportunity to bring their crippled friend to Jesus. They came with enormous faith. Faith in what Jesus could do. Faith in their own ability to break through the crowd, the roof and the meeting in order to bring their friend to him.

In that moment, Jesus said the unexpected. Instead of saying "stand up and walk," he said that the man's sins were forgiven. He knew the impact of those words. He knew that it would make things even more difficult for him. He knew that he was pronouncing who he was to those who would carry the news back to the leaders and priests.

Afterwards, he went out to tell the good news to the people and ran into Levi (Matthew), a tax collector. This time he went and ate at Levi's house with his "sinful" friends. When questioned, he announced more good news. He had come for the sinners, the broken, the sick. God was sending His Son to forgive sins and heal. The Kingdom of God had truly come near.

What will it take for you to hear the good news, to share it? Maybe you already get it. Maybe you are praying for those who don't. Do you want to be like the four friends, strong enough in your faith to break through the barriers in order to get their friend to Jesus? Do you want to be like Levi, who changed his life by one step of faith? Maybe you just want to be a good witness to your family or friends who don't know Jesus yet.

Take a minute to ask yourself what holds you back. What is it that keeps you from sharing a word, touching a heart, reaching out to someone in need? What is it that stops you from being a "faith-full" friend? Why not pray about it and ask God for more faith, more willingness, more boldness? Why not step out in one way today so that someone you know can hear about Jesus and be saved?

Journal your thoughts:

_____

_____

_____

_____

_____

_____

_____

_____

_____

_____

_____

_____

_____

_____

_____

Blinders
Mark 2:18-3:6

Here we find Jesus being questioned about his actions and the actions of his disciples. Why don't they fast? Why do you work on the Sabbath? Why are you acting contrary to our laws?

It is so easy to take something good and make it so rigid that it becomes a problem. So it was with the law. You should fast, you should rest, you should obey. Yes, yes and yes. But here Jesus sets up some realities. We don't fast when there is a celebration, when the "One" has come and is teaching us. We don't hold onto things just because "we've always done it that way". We don't let the need for rest keep us from being kind and caring, from taking care of needs, whether physical or spiritual.

Realizing that Jesus was the New Wine, the Compassionate Servant, we can see that changes were required. The Pharisees had gotten mired in the law to the point that they stopped seeing the people, the needs. The new way is love and compassion. The new way is seeing all time as sacred, all actions as worship.

Fasting is good. It takes us out of ourselves and our earthly needs for a time, but there is a time for it. Resting on the Sabbath needs to happen more in our culture, but even now, there are times when expressions of compassion are more important.

I was thinking, what is it that I hold onto, that keeps me from being like Jesus? Is it an unspoken rule in my mind? Is it a "law" that I practice without regard for those around me? Is it that I have gotten so focused on the tiniest thing that I have missed the point? The Pharisees were like that. They couldn't see the truth – Messiah was in their midst! They couldn't see the need – we are hungry. They couldn't see the hurt – my arm is useless. They had blinders on because they were so focused on what not to do.

Jesus said, "The Sabbath was made for man (2:27)." God knew we would need a day of rest, a day set apart. It wasn't made for rules but for refreshing.

What blinders keep you from seeing the needs around you? What "rule" holds you back from caring for someone in need? Consider Jesus, who ate with sinners, healed the broken, celebrated with friends. Let your life look like his. It is all he asks.

Journal your thoughts:

_____

_____

_____

_____

_____

_____

_____

_____

_____

_____

_____

_____

_____

_____

_____

_____

Hearing the News
Mark 3:7-19

They came from all over, from both sides of the Jordan River to see and hear Jesus. They traveled to him, probably walking for days to get there. So many came that he had to speak to them from a boat. I often imagine the crowds, listening, hoping to be able to hear or touch him. I imagine those who had already followed him watching in amazement while Jesus spoke the good news. It must have been exhausting and exhilarating at the same time.

Then there were the evil spirits, those that possessed some in the crowd. They cried out, but he silenced them because it wasn't time to declare his mission. Still, many heard and knew. Confusion, chaos, high emotions all caused him to choose to be a few feet away, to separate himself as much as he could. They needed him. They needed to hear his message, but even Jesus couldn't keep it up continuously.

So, he went away with the twelve. He called them apostles, which means messengers, so that they too could take the message, so that they could share the load. Do you hear what that means? Even Jesus didn't do it alone. As the Son of God, he had the power to do so, but he didn't choose to do that. Instead he called them - and he called us - to do the work alongside him. I don't know about you, but I find that amazing. And they must have too. We hear later of bickering but at this moment they must have all been so amazed that he chose them.

While Mark doesn't share the disciples' response with us, we can imagine some ways they might have reacted. What would you have done? Would you have knelt before him? Would you have wanted to hug him? Would you have cried out, "why me?" or cheered? It must have been an amazing moment for these disciples of Jesus.

It might be good to take a minute today to remember your amazing moment, the moment when you realized Jesus loved you and wanted you for his team. Maybe you were a little child, but you finally knew Jesus loved you. Maybe it happened later in your life and everything changed. It feels good to get picked for the team.

I hope you can spend some time today standing on the beach, listening to Jesus share the news. I hope you spend some time today thanking him that he called you to be his. I hope you spend a moment today offering thanksgiving to God for His Son. How blessed we are to know him and to serve him.

Go! Tell someone the good news!

Journal your thoughts:

_____

_____

_____

_____

_____

_____

_____

_____

_____

_____

_____

_____

_____

_____

By the Spirit of God
Mark 3:20-35

This is where the "rubber meets the road" for Jesus. Accused of having an evil spirit, he has to take a stand against this grievous sin – blaspheming against the Holy Spirit. He has to choose between family and truth, between the "chosen people" and the broken, wounded sinners that were following him. It must have hurt his God-sized heart to have to speak so harshly.

Satan wants to divide us, to damage our connections to the true Spirit of God. Jesus wants to bring us together to serve – together. Families fight, they break apart, but this is not God's doing. Jesus stood in full opposition to the "evil spirits." How could the leaders, then, accuse him of being part of them? It amazes me how hard Satan works to mess with our minds.

I've often wondered what "blaspheming the Spirit" really meant but I see it here and understand. When Jesus was baptized, the Holy Spirit descended on him (Mark 1:10). When the teachers and family members said he had a different spirit, they were denying what was already known, that is, Jesus was filled with only one Spirit, the Spirit of God. To say otherwise was to call God a liar. Harsh indeed.

Yet Jesus wanted us to understand this: we are his family. If we seek him, if we follow him, if we listen at his feet, we are his. We are his brothers and sisters, sons and daughters. By faith we are related to him. We are his. If you are worried that you have committed the unpardonable sin, know that you probably haven't done so. Though your past attitude toward Jesus might have been negative, you need to know that all who come to him are saved and accepted. Rejecting him is the only unforgiveable sin.

Amazing! He took our sins in order to add us to his family. He took our place in order to become our friend, our brother. He took our hurt, our wounds, our broken places so that we could be healed and be joined to his Kingdom work. What a mighty God we serve!

Journal your thoughts:

_____

_____

_____

_____

_____

_____

_____

_____

_____

_____

_____

_____

_____

_____

_____

Types of Soil
Mark 4:1-25

In dealing with the parables of Jesus, we need to be reminded, again and again, that there are ways that we miss the point. Here Jesus is telling the people that God's ways, His Kingdom, are not easily understood. We may think we see or understand, but we are often off base and far from the mark. Jesus wants us to get it but understanding the things of God only comes from God through the Holy Spirit. Trying to understand on our own doesn't work.

How did the word of God get planted in you? Did you struggle with it? Did you hear it but never let it in? Did you have so many earthly worries and plans that it couldn't take hold of your heart? Or did you take it into your heart and begin to spread the good news around?

We often have to hear something more than once to understand its importance, its relevance in our lives. We are told by our parents that things are "hot" and not to touch, but we often don't want to listen, we often try it "just once more" to see if they are right. It's the same way with God's word. We may have read it or heard it in our lives, but it never was any more important than any other words. We may have even memorized a psalm or saying, but it never really touched us.

This is the parable of the soils. When you first heard the word, was it so unimportant to you that Satan could snatch it away from you? Were you so loaded with other cares and heartaches that there was no space for it? Or did you allow it in so that it could change you and help you to find that close relationship that God wants with each of his children?

Whatever happened that first time, or second, or third, it is never too late to let God's word "dwell in you richly" (Colossians 3:16). Never too late to heed the words of Jesus and come to him, follow him. The "Sower" will continually work the soil in your life, so that the seeds that continue to come to you may take root and flourish. All he asks is that you open your heart and let the word enter.

"Today, if you hear his voice, do not harden your hearts" (Hebrews 4:7). Instead, we should open our hearts and minds to his word, so that we will produce a crop worthy of the Lord.

Journal your thoughts:

_____

_____

_____

_____

_____

_____

_____

_____

_____

_____

_____

_____

_____

_____

Don't You Care?
Mark 4:26-41

"Teacher, don't you care?" It is the age-old question. Does God really care about us, about our little lives, our messes, our needs? Do you ever wonder if He does?

The disciples had spent the day learning about the Kingdom, how it was going to work, grow, become what God had planted. We see that God uses small things to do large things. He uses good soil, and he cares for that soil so that the plants (us) may grow strong and useful to His work. The disciples sat right there and listened to him share his parables. Not only that but they got the inside scoop, the explanations, the clear message.

So why, only a few hours later would they ask if Jesus cared? Was anything too big for him? Obviously, they needed to see beyond their preconceived notions to the reality. Jesus wasn't worried, he was asleep. He had no fear. Nothing – nothing was too big for God. His faith as a human, his understanding as part of the Godhead, all combined to make him calm in the midst of the storm.

Not so the disciples. Not so with us. The storms come and, like the disciples, we run crying to Jesus, "Don't you care?" Don't you care that my child is sick? Don't you care that I can't pay my bills? Don't you care that our church is struggling? Don't you care that our world is a mess? Don't you care?

And he says to the wind, and he says to us, "Quiet, be still" (vs. 39). Not so that everything will change in an instant, but so that our hearts can hear him speaking, "Be still and know that I am God" (Psalm 46:10). BE STILL. We are so often too busy to hear, too busy to be quiet, too busy to know that he cares for us. He cares about our storms and he speaks.

What is your storm today? Be still and wait on the Lord. Listen for his voice reminding you to quiet down and have faith because he cares.

Journal your thoughts:

_____

_____

_____

_____

_____

_____

_____

_____

_____

_____

_____

_____

_____

_____

_____

_____

Tell Your Family
Mark 5:1-20

Picture it. You have arrived after a rough trip across the sea. Who meets you? A person who appears crazed, probably with scars, dirty and out of his mind. What would you do when this person comes running toward your leader, screaming at him? Would you try and stop him? Would you stand and stare? What would he see in your eyes? Disgust? Fear?

We will never know what the disciples did or thought. They'd just gotten off the boat after Jesus had calmed the water. They might still have been in shock over that. In any case, they were, once again, observers of the power of Jesus.

Now imagine you are the man possessed. Within you rages not just one but many evil spirits. They've even named themselves "Legion." You are not in control of what you do, not in your right mind. The rage, the destructive thoughts drive you. And then, HE comes, and Legion finally meets its match.

What does it feel like to come to your senses? To be in your right mind after a long dark time? What does it feel like to know the healing power of Jesus, whether in mind or body? All of us have been changed by Jesus. It may not be this dramatic, but our lives finally come into focus as he calls us to himself and saves us from our sins. We, like this man, have been on a wrong path, locked in a struggle of wills.

What is your response? The man sat down with Jesus and

listened. Calmed by his presence, he began acting normally. He took time to listen and learn. He wanted to go with Jesus, to stay with the one who had made him whole.

Instead, he was given a mission. "Go home to your family and tell them how much the Lord has done for you, and how he has had mercy on you (Mark 5:19)." This is our mission too. Begin with your family, tell them what has happened, and then, like this man, go to your neighbors, your town, your region and beyond and tell them too. The world needs to be "amazed" by what Jesus has done in your life. How will they know if we don't tell them what Jesus has done for us?

Journal your thoughts:

_____

_____

_____

_____

_____

_____

_____

_____

_____

_____

_____

_____

_____

_____

_____

Healing, Please!
Mark 5:21-43

It's all about Jesus. There they were again, waiting for him. "Jesus is coming back! I see the boat!" They waited. Some wanted to see what all this was about. Some wanted to see him perform miracles. Some wanted to learn from him, "teacher," "rabbi." For some it was a moment of excitement, a chance to see or do something new. And so, they waited, wondering what came next.

On this day, there were two in the crowd who were desperate. Two who came for help and in hope. They couldn't have been more different. One, a synagogue leader, the other a woman, unclean due to her illness. One was bold enough to come forward and plead his case, the other fearful to be seen. For each of them, there was only one thought: healing. "Please Jesus, heal my child." "Heal me."

It always surprises me that Jesus stopped to find the woman. After all, healing the child of a synagogue leader might have helped his cause, should have been his first priority. Yet he stopped.

Andy Stanley reminds us in the study "Simple" that "Jesus liked people who weren't like him." I love that. Jesus liked the sinners and the unclean. He cared for the broken and the totally messed up people. AND he cared for the leaders and their children.

Much of what is said about this passage is about faith, faith to believe that healing is possible. But it is about so much more. It is about who Jesus is, the compassionate Shepherd who cares for all his sheep. It is about the love of God for those who are on the outside of society, as well as for those who are in with the "in crowd." It is about delayed answers, fear, joy.

Why do you come to see Jesus? Is it for the show? For healing? To learn something? Or is it because of who he is? Maybe you are still skeptical, and you walk away from the crowd confused and doubtful. Don't stop coming. Each time you encounter Jesus, you will learn, see, understand more. He will stop and look for you – yes, you – and you will see him for who he is: Mighty God, Prince of Peace, Gentle Shepherd. So just keep coming. He's waiting for you.

Journal your thoughts:

_____

_____

_____

_____

_____

_____

_____

_____

_____

_____

_____

_____

_____

_____

_____

Rejection
Mark 6:1-29

What is it about going home? No matter what we experienced as children, good or bad, going home is always a difficult experience. Recently, I attended my 50th reunion. It was great, but as with most of us, I worried about what would happen, who would show up, would they like who I am now. Jesus might have wondered what the reaction might be when he went home.

The carpenter's son, the brother, the "odd" child who was Mary's firstborn. How would the changes in him be received? The Scripture says, "they took offense." Really? Offended by the way he had grown into a man of God? Offended by his miracles, his wisdom? Offended by what exactly? But that's the point. Often, people who don't know Jesus are offended by him. Maybe you have the same problem with your family – "Who does she think she is?" "Wasn't he the one who...?" We change but those who knew us best can't see it or don't like it. How hard it must have been for Jesus to be rejected by his own people.

Lack of faith blinds people to the truth. Miracles could not happen in certain places. The twelve were able to cast out demons, but not all. What about you? Do you allow what you knew in the past to impact how you react to someone now? Do you struggle to believe that they have changed? Do you put your perceptions onto someone so that you cannot see them for who they are? Even

Herod wanted to believe that Jesus was someone else, raised from the dead.

I love that God puts the doubters and the broken people in the Bible. We can learn so much from those in Jesus' home town. First, allow for change in people you know. Be open to seeing what God has done in a life, small or large changes, all are important. Second, don't expect everyone will understand how you've changed. Forgive them and move on. And third, speak the truth anyway. Don't let the naysayers stop you from growing and changing even more. You are becoming – day by day.

If you were to go home now, what changes would people see in you? And would they believe what they see?

Embrace the changes

Journal your thoughts:

_____

_____

_____

_____

_____

_____

_____

_____

_____

_____

_____

_____

_____

_____

_____

Overload
Mark 6:30-56

It must have been exhausting! Wherever he went, they followed. Whenever he tried to get away, they were there. Hungry, broken, sick, paralyzed, they came hoping for the cure, for the miracle that would change their lives.

Think of how overwhelming it must have seemed to the disciples. Their minds were overloaded with the things they saw, the people, the expectations. Day after day, no matter where they went, they were surrounded by needy people. Can you imagine? Here is Peter, who had spent his life quietly fishing, now trying to get away from all those people, just for a few minutes.

We can talk about the feeding of 5000 people – miracle. Or the healings of many – more miracles. We can talk all we want about how amazing it was to be there, to be healed or fed. But can we talk for a minute about overload? Why had the hearts of the disciples become hard? Why do ours? Because we can't take it all in. The needs, so many needs. The heartbreaking stories of pain and sorrow. The masses of people following just to get a look or a touch from Jesus. And we ourselves have needs, don't we?

So here they are, out in the boat, in another storm, and this time, Jesus isn't even with them. What were they thinking? They'd weathered storms before, they could handle this? Or maybe, Jesus helped everyone else, why isn't he here? Or how about this one, after we've been so faithful, he sends another storm our way? Isn't this what we think? Where is he when I need him?

It isn't such a big surprise that they don't recognize him walking toward them. Their minds are not in the right place, nor are their hearts. How patient Jesus is with them. How patient he is with us. He continues to show us who he is. And we are amazed, again.

It's time to open up our minds and hearts to the truth. Jesus is who he said he is. He uses the phrase "ego emi" which means "It is I," or "I am." These are the same words that God uses to describe himself in the Old Testament. Jesus isn't just telling the disciples that he is here for them now, but that he is always here, he IS continually, for all time and space. He is telling them to open up their understanding to the fact that Jesus is God. He knows it will take time for this to sink in, but he continues to show them his power and his compassion.

How patient, how understanding is our Lord, that he would continually open our hearts and minds to the truth of who he is. He is the bread of life, the living vine, the alpha and omega, the Good Shepherd. When he says, "I am," he wants us to embrace that fully.

Take a minute today to let all that sink in. The one who fed 5000 people on a hillside is the one who cares about your needs, your storms, your pain. HE IS, always and forever and, therefore, he will be with you through it all.

Journal your thoughts:

_____

_____

_____

_____

_____

_____

_____

_____

_____

_____

_____

_____

_____

_____

_____

_____

_____

It's About the Heart
Mark 7:1-23

In our germ conscious culture, it might seem strange that Jesus wouldn't agree with the teachers about washing hands before eating, but he never said it wasn't a good practice. The teachers were all about the rules, over six-hundred of them. Some came from the ten commandments, but many were just "traditions" that had been created to teach and guide. Some of those traditions had become more important that the true laws of God.

In the battle between Jesus and the teachers, there was one clear message: It is about the heart, about love. The little rules and traditions aren't necessarily wrong, but the method of guilting people and taking them to the extreme is. And putting tradition over really important things is wrong.

We've talked about traditions before. Nothing wrong with those if they don't become your focus, if they don't become legalism. The ten commandments covered all that we need to understand about how to treat people and possessions. And Jesus took it a little further to show us that the law is there to point out our need for God. No matter what we do, we are totally able to mess it up!

What is it for you? What little rule gets first place in your actions? Do you do it because you always did? Or have you put it in context and examined whether it truly is something that is important? Some rules are given for us as we grow up and then they don't apply anymore. Some are given to help us live better. What matters is whether those ideas line up with the law of love and whether our hearts are lined up with those actions.

Food enters and leaves our bodies daily. The attitudes of the heart are there inside, leading us one way or the other. So, I ask you, how is your heart today? What traditions or attitudes might be hindering you from living a life for God? What thoughts hold you back from loving your neighbor? What really needs washing in your life?

I think I need to go do some "house cleaning" – have a blessed day.

Journal your thoughts:

_____

_____

_____

_____

_____

_____

_____

_____

_____

_____

_____

_____

_____

_____

_____

_____

Interruptions
Mark 7: 24-37

Does Jesus sometimes sound harsh to you? Here is just another person, looking for help, for healing and he says, "First let the children eat all they want, for it is not right to take the children's bread and toss it to the dogs" (vs. 27). If you were a person that took offense easily, you would think that he is calling names. "You aren't even fit to eat at the table with the children," you might think. Or, "who is he to call me a dog?"

Instead of reacting in anger, this woman points out a truth. Even the dogs get the crumbs. Brilliant!

There is a point to what Jesus said. He had come to bring his people back to God. The "children" he is talking about are the Jews. Paul said, "first to the Jew and then the Gentile." Jesus had only so much time and he had to use it where it would count. He wasn't calling the woman a dog. He was referring to her nationality – Gentile. And yet, she answered him with intelligence and grace. "Just a few crumbs for my child?"

Do you ever get so focused that you miss the potential ministry that's right next to you? While Jesus was fully aware of all that went on around him, I think he was probably focused on something important when this woman showed up. We don't know what he was talking about, but it is likely that his statement to her fit in with the discussion he was having. He had to shift gears in order to hear her request.

What do you do with interruptions? Do you get frustrated? Snarky? Do you brush them aside and continue on your way? This woman didn't let that happen. Her need was too great. Maybe there is someone in your life who has been pulling on your shirttails or begging for a moment of your time. What have you done? Do you step out of your own space and into theirs? Jesus did, and the people continued to come and to tell others.

Why not take a moment today for that person who needs you? Listen to them. Hear their heart. Pray with them and let them know that you care. If you don't, you might miss a God-given opportunity to share the good news, to spread the word that "Jesus is amazing."

Why not think of someone that needs your prayers. Send them a note or an email telling them that you prayed for them.

Journal your thoughts:

_____

_____

_____

_____

_____

_____

_____

_____

_____

_____

_____

_____

_____

_____

_____

_____

Missing the Point
Mark 8:1-21

We laughed at the disciples in our Bible Study yesterday, but we were laughing at ourselves too. How often do we acknowledge God in our lives one day and then wonder where He is the next? Are we any different than the disciples, who should have "seen" and "understood" what was happening?

Both Matthew and Mark mention a second feeding miracle. I wonder if it didn't happen more times than we know. The people were constantly coming, in crowds. Perhaps there were many such miracles. But even if there were only two, surely the disciples would begin to understand the power of Jesus, who he was. Yet, like us, they missed the point. They were so focused on earthly things, like bread, that they couldn't see the spiritual implications of all that they saw.

"Do you still not understand?" Do you? Do I? What will it take for us to truly believe?

The Pharisees asked for a sign. Understand that they didn't want another spectacular miracle. They wanted a "sign," something worthy of the Prophets. They wanted real proof of his authority, a sign from heaven. Jesus essentially tells them that they wouldn't recognize one if they saw it, and that they weren't going to get one because of their unbelief. How frustrated they must have been. They wanted to trick him into doing something, but he wasn't fooled.

All the signs that were needed had already been given, through the prophets. Matthew mentions the "sign of Jonah" as the only sign they would receive. So, how many more miracles or signs did the disciples need to finally, completely understand? We're only on Chapter 8, so we know it takes some more time.

You and I have the "rest of the story" already. We know what the disciples eventually learned, what they shared with the world, what they were willing to die for. We have the truth. Do we still not understand? Are we still looking at earthly things, letting the worries and hardships of the world consume our thoughts or are we ready to step out in faith to advance the Kingdom of God?

Today, as you go about your everyday tasks, think about this: What is one thing I can do today to live by faith? How can I show one person that Jesus is really who he said he is?

It's time to step out in faith.

Journal your thoughts:

_____

_____

_____

_____

_____

_____

_____

_____

_____

_____

_____

_____

_____

_____

_____

Acceptance
Mark 8:22-38

Today's word is acceptance. We talk about it in the area of grief when we slowly move on and accept what has happened, letting go of the wishful thinking. When we finally accept the circumstances of our life, we can begin to see the potential for the future.

In this passage, Jesus continues to open up to the disciples, pushing their former notions and beliefs to the side so that they can see him clearly. It is amazing that they "got it" but didn't really get it at all. It was more of a wish than a belief, when Peter stated the Jesus was the Messiah. What got in his way was the understanding of the mission. Messiah was going to come and change everything – right? He was going to come and be the new ruler, here and now. That's what Peter had been taught, that's what he hoped for.

So now, after all these miracles, all these examples of his power, Jesus tells them he is going to die. WHAT? No that's not how it's supposed to work. I think I would have stood right next to Peter when he rebuked Jesus. I wouldn't have been able to wrap my brain around such an idea.

Do you have in mind the things of God? Do you push aside ideas and plans that don't meet with your "earthly" ideals? I know that I have done so. Jeremiah 29:11 says, "For I know the plans I have for you," declares the LORD, "plans to prosper you and not to harm you, plans to give you hope and a future." We quote that often, but do we really want the plans that God has for us?

Jesus makes it clear. These things you must do: let go of the life you planned and take on the one God planned. Deny yourself. Remember it's not about you, it's about the Kingdom of God. Take up your cross. Whatever hardship you have been through, however difficult your life, there is something in it that Jesus can use. Don't carry it as a burden, carry it into the world so that you can help others in the same kind of situation. Follow. Jesus may lead us on difficult paths, but remember, he is leading, we just need to follow him through.

Finally, wear your faith boldly. Stand up for Jesus, for the hope that we have in him. Stand tall and firm because the world needs to know.

Journal your thoughts:

_____

_____

_____

_____

_____

_____

_____

_____

_____

_____

_____

_____

_____

_____

_____

_____

Revelation
Mark 9:1-13

Imagine yourself standing on a mountain with Jesus and two of your closest friends. He picked the three of you to see something, learn something. He said that some of your group would not see death before they saw the Kingdom come. Your mind is full of so much that he has told you and you want to understand. Suddenly, Jesus is changed. He is radiant and glorious. And Elijah and Moses appear with him. You've seen miracles, but this? How does a person take this in and understand it?

Even though Peter has been rebuked for not accepting the fact that Jesus has to die, he still hopes that Jesus will be around for a long time. He therefore offers to build some shelters for the three. Was it fear that made him speak? Was it hope? Peter tended to blurt out the first thing that came to his mind, and this was it. "Let's settle down for a long time of fellowship and sharing." Afraid or not, Peter wanted this experience to go on forever. Wouldn't you?

Then came the cloud and the voice. Here is God, revealing his plan to these three. The cloud, just like the one that lead the Israelites in the wilderness, descends on Jesus, Elijah and Moses. And the voice, did it thunder? Was it still and small? Whatever it sounded like, they heard it. "This is my Son whom I love. Listen to him." And then it was gone. All of it, the radiance, the others, the cloud, the voice and Jesus stood before them alone.

Take it in. Be still with that picture for a few minutes.

The words "This is my Son" put all the pieces together. Sonship was declared as Jesus stood with Moses, who represented the Law, and Elijah, who represented the prophets. The Son stands alone above the Law and the Prophets. Here, in a nutshell, is the truth. Jesus is Messiah. He is the Son. It is his Kingdom that is near.

"Listen to him." To them that word meant listen, learn and obey. Keep listening and act on what you learn. This is the call of a disciple. This is our call.

One last time, Jesus tells them not to tell anyone yet, and they don't, but they have so many questions. You can read the rest. All has been fulfilled. From this moment forward, the push is toward the crucifixion, death and resurrection.

Glory be to God!

Journal your thoughts:

_____

_____

_____

_____

_____

_____

_____

_____

_____

_____

_____

_____

_____

_____

_____

_____

Unbelief
Mark 9:14-32

"If you can..." Oh, Lord, help our unbelief. It seems like no matter how many times Jesus performed a miracle, people still questioned his ability. I guess we do that too, don't we? We pray and then we decide he either doesn't care or he can't do what we ask. Now don't get me wrong, sometimes we ask for things that he doesn't think are good for us. Sometimes he says no or not yet. But to question whether he is willing... I guess it's human nature.

So here is this parent whose child is possessed. The disciples try to deal with it. After all, they've driven out spirits before. To their surprise, it doesn't work. Something is not right, and then Jesus returns to find everyone confused and frustrated.

Of course, the father is going to question whether Jesus can or will do this. He has asked for help, probably over and over, with no results. Not even the disciples of Jesus could deal with this one. But he didn't give up. He went straight to the source, boldly stating his concern. "Are you willing?" "Will you do this for my child?" It was his last hope.

Have you reached a place of "last hope?" Maybe a sick child or family member. Maybe a besetting sin or addiction. Maybe a financial crisis. Jesus is willing to help. He is willing to work with you, to guide and direct you. He is willing.

So, what does he mean that this kind can only come out by prayer? I think the message here is that we tend to get ahead of ourselves. We prayed yesterday, or the last time, and it worked, but we forgot to pray this time. The disciples probably felt that way. "We did it before, we can do it again." Over and over again we are reminded to rely on God, to ask him for his power and his strength. And over and over, we rely on ourselves and our past successes.

Have you prayed for something? Pray again. Do you need healing? Pray again. Keep the lines open to God. Never doubt that he cares.

We do believe, Lord. Help us overcome our unbelief.

Journal your thoughts:

_____

_____

_____

_____

_____

_____

_____

_____

_____

_____

_____

_____

_____

_____

_____

Servanthood
Mark 9:33-50

We don't like to talk about it, much less consider the consequences. One of the wonderful things about Jesus is that he doesn't hold back. What is it? Sin. And how our actions hurt not only us but others. Whatever it is that causes us to sin or "stumble" needs to be dealt with. And if we cause someone else to sin, we are really in trouble.

How do we deal with these very serious statements? Do we make our lives all about doing good? Do we actually cut off a hand or cut out an eye?

Here, Jesus is talking about the one who has been driving out demons. He is not yet "one of them," but he obviously has some faith in who Jesus might be. In taking the little child on his lap, Jesus is pointing out a serious lesson. As disciples, they had to treat others as they would a child, even someone who might be acting outside of the fold. To scold or rebuke might "cause them to sin," cause them to turn away from Jesus.

When we think about the disciples, we often see them as a rag-tag bunch of misfits who are continually missing the point. That they are, but they are also God's choice to spread the good news. Every lesson, every point Jesus makes is for their future work. He teaches, explains and then does it again. Over and over, he uses different illustrations to teach the same points. "This is what it looks like to be my disciples."

Be kind. Treat others like Jesus treated the children. Don't be too harsh on those who are trying to understand. Be salt, bringing flavor to the world around you.

Jesus asked them what they were talking about, but he knew. Peter, James and John had just been singled out to experience the transfiguration. They were probably boasting, like little kids: "He picked me!" But Jesus uses their pride to express his most important teaching. "Be a servant." This is what he wants from all of us.

In the end, it's not about what sins we commit. Sin is sin. It is about how our lives impact our world and sin simply gets in the way. In all things, we are to be servants, humble, kind, and salty. And finally, we are to be at peace with one another. What a world this would be if we only followed this plan!

Journal your thoughts:

_____

_____

_____

_____

_____

_____

_____

_____

_____

_____

_____

_____

_____

_____

_____

_____

Mindset
Mark 10:1-16

What is your attitude toward God? Seriously, do you want to take what you like from God but ignore the rest? Do you truly trust that God has your best in mind?

At the end of this passage, Jesus tells the disciples that they need the mind – attitude – of a little child. Children are so trusting. They do what adults tell them. They believe their parents love them. They want to please. It's so open and honest with kids, even in disobedience. Adults, on the other hand, have to carefully use their words. We care about how we look to others, how we are perceived. We care about so much stuff that doesn't matter in the end.

Because of our self-protective nature, relationships get broken, people get hurt and we run away. I've been there and maybe you have too. Marriage is tough. Relationships are tough. Maintaining them is a full-time job. Jesus wants us to try and to keep trying. His teaching here is tough. Work on it. (As an aside, there is grace over all broken relationships.) God began with a plan. We have messed it up. If you are married, keep at it. If your relationship has broken up, make sure you've done all you can to fix it. If you are remarried, work on that one. (Disclaimer: Jesus continued to point us back to what was best, to the truth about marriage and many other things. I do not, however, believe that he wanted us to stay in abusive or dangerous relationships. Get help if that is what you are dealing with.)

In the end, it's our attitude – ours. It's about how we deal with each other, how we love. In a perfect world, our children would be perfect, our marriages would be perfect, our friendships would be perfect. In a perfect world, people would be perfect. But we aren't. We can, however, have a good attitude toward our children, our spouses, our friends and yes, even our enemies.

One of the wonderful things about kids is that they can hate each other one day and love each other the next. We need to be like that. Are you angry today? Cool down and wait it out. Have you been hurt? God can heal that wound.

A good attitude can take you a long way in this crazy world. Why not work on *your* attitude and let God work on everyone else.

Journal your thoughts:

_____

_____

_____

_____

_____

_____

_____

_____

_____

_____

_____

_____

_____

_____

_____

_____

Letting Go
Mark 10:17-34

"He went away sad." Many people say that being a Christian is a crutch, just a way to make yourself feel better, but when you look at this story you realize that it isn't like that at all. Sure, believing in God gives us hope for the future. It makes us feel like someone is on our side. But it is so much more than that.

What have you had to give up for God? The rich young man thought he had done all the right things, and Jesus loved him for it, but there was one thing holding him back from truly trusting in God. For him it was his wealth, he just couldn't let it go. For you it might be your family or your high position. Maybe it's your comfortable lifestyle or your place in the community. What do you need to give up in order to truly follow Jesus?

Peter and the others gave up their livelihood, Levi his income. Paul gave up everything he had been trained to be.

A pastor of mine once demonstrated what was needed by walking across the platform and then turning around 180°. This is the change that happens when we decide to live for Jesus. It is not a crutch. It is a commitment of our whole lives to a different direction, a different way of living.

When I became a Christian, my father was extremely upset, for you see my relatives are all humanists. Their faith is in humanity and science. For them to follow Christ would require them to tear out the fiber of all they have based their lives on. And it may be so for you. Maybe you are reading this because someone told you it was good. Maybe you are searching to understand a friend who believes. For whatever reason you are reading this today, I ask again: What is God asking you to let go of so that you can truly follow him?

Another question might be, what is God asking you to do? Where might he want you to go? Are you willing? It's hard for us, in our comfortable little houses, in our comfortable little neighborhoods, to let go and begin to live for Christ. Maybe, like my friends who are returning to the mission field after 20 years at a church here, you need to step up your game. I know I might need to do the same.

I hope you don't "walk away sad" from this message. Rather, ponder it, consider what God is asking of you and be ready to go in that direction. And may he bless your efforts.

Journal your thoughts:

_____

_____

_____

_____

_____

_____

_____

_____

_____

_____

_____

_____

_____

_____

_____

Choose Me
Mark 10:35-52

Maybe James and John thought they had something that the other disciples didn't. Maybe they thought they were smarter or stronger. They certainly had guts to ask Jesus their question. I don't think I would have done it, and yet, in some ways, we all ask this. "Can I be the one closest to you?" "Pick me!"

Jesus is very clear. "You don't know what you are asking." He wanted to make it clear to them that closeness to him meant hard work and pain. To get where they wanted to go, they had to endure what he did, fight for what they believed and die for it. "Can you drink the cup?" "We can."

There are times to ask the bold questions and times to keep quiet. James and John got the lesson that Jesus had been teaching all along: "Be a servant." We all like to be at the top. We want people to like us. Many of us want to have positions that elevate us, put us higher than others. Some of us want to be CEO or president of something, but Jesus wants us to consider a different path, the path of a servant.

Greatness, in Jesus' economy, comes from being last. It is the idea that others are more important than you, that being one who serves is better than being served. In the Kingdom of God, service is the key. It is shown in how the Trinity lifts each other up. Jesus points us to the Father and the Father to Jesus. The Holy Spirit elevates Jesus and Jesus does the same for the Holy Spirit. Our goal is to be like them, lifting others up.

As Jesus moves from this discussion, he once again heals someone. He puts aside the thoughts of glory to humble himself and help a blind beggar because it's not about him, it's about love and grace and servanthood. It's about the Kingdom coming on earth. For that to happen, we must live out love and grace and compassion.

How are you doing in this? Are you self-glorifying or self-effacing? Do you want to be lifted up by others or do you want them to be lifted up? Are you living a Kingdom life as servant of all?

Journal your thoughts:

_____

_____

_____

_____

_____

_____

_____

_____

_____

_____

_____

_____

_____

_____

_____

_____

The King is Coming
Mark 11:1-19

A colt, a fig tree and the moneychangers. All of these are setting up what is to come, pointing out how broken Israel was and what was needed.

There are so many questions. How did Jesus know about the colt? Did he plan to have it there or was it a supernatural knowledge? Did the owner understand that Jesus was referring to himself as Lord? Did the people? Why the fig tree? Why was he so angry?

It is likely that this was a prophetic moment and that Jesus knew that entering into Jerusalem on a donkey, as conquering kings often did, indicated Kingship. The people began to lay down a carpet of coats and branches for his steed to walk on and cried out words from the prophetic psalm (118).

Did they really know who he was? Many did. Did they really understand his purpose? Most didn't. Nonetheless, they cheered and cried out for a savior. Hosanna means "save us now." After years of exile and then years under Roman rule, the people were ready to be saved. The Messiah had come to help them, hadn't he?

For some reason, the story of the fig tree is placed here in Mark's narrative. Here is a tree that looks like it should have fruit but doesn't. As with many of Jesus actions, the fig tree probably represents something else. Many scholars suggest that it represents Israel, which, while looking good, was not bearing the fruit it was supposed to. This prophetic action declared that Israel would no longer be the focal point of God's message. Indeed, the cursing of the tree was not because Jesus was mad at the tree but because he saw Israel's hypocrisy.

As for the money-changers, Jesus' reaction was similar. God's house had been defiled. The way into the temple had become congested, keeping people out of the court of the Gentiles. Once again, Jesus shows his frustration with those who are supposed to be drawing people to the One True God.

In hindsight, the disciples understood the importance of it all. The Kingdom had come near. The King had arrived. Not the political king, but the gentle, humble king, riding on a donkey. The King who wanted people to be able to enter his courts freely. The King who had come to shake things up, to return the hearts of the people to God.

"Blessed is He who comes in the Name of the Lord."

Journal your thoughts:

_____

_____

_____

_____

_____

_____

_____

_____

_____

_____

_____

_____

_____

_____

_____

_____

Moving Mountains
Mark 11:20-33

Faith, it's everything. Whatever mountain needs to be moved, whatever crisis needs solving, it's all about faith. Do you believe that God can and will answer prayer? As the disciples get closer and closer to understanding, Jesus once again uses the fig tree to teach them. He spoke to the tree and it withered and died. He spoke to the storm and it calmed down. He spoke a prayer over the fish and the loaves, and they multiplied.

So how is your faith? Do you have enough to move a mountain? A mound? An anthill?

Jesus wants us to strengthen our faith, believing in who he is and what he can do. As he entered the temple, the leaders accosted him with questions. "By what authority?" In other words, "Who do you think you are?" This is a question we all need to answer in our heart. Who was he really? Does he really mean that I can move mountains? Does he really come from God?

Part of our faith journey is to come to grips with what is true. The Pharisees couldn't, or wouldn't, accept Jesus because he didn't fit in their box or follow their plans. Our faith only goes as far as we are willing to set aside our plans for his, our kingdom for his. Until we do, we can only go so far.

Where are you in your journey? Are you just beginning, pondering the miracles and wondering about his teaching? Are you wrestling with God over the way you want things to be? Or are you settled in the truth that his plans are better, his path is safer?

Why not spend some time today making sure that you are on a firm foundation and building for the Kingdom of God? Then, pray about what you think he wants, and he will answer. Go and bear much fruit.

Journal your thoughts:

_____

_____

_____

_____

_____

_____

_____

_____

_____

_____

_____

_____

_____

_____

_____

_____

_____

It's All His
Mark 12:1-17

So many things keep us from getting the message of Jesus, the heir, the son. The tenants in this parable don't want to pay up. They don't want to live the way tenants are supposed to live. They want it their way and they made a decision to take what wasn't theirs.

We get so comfortable in our lives that we often miss the main theme: God with us. And so, when the son came to collect from them, they didn't want to face facts. They didn't want to live by the rules of tenancy. Their pride and arrogance brought them down.

The Pharisees knew they were in a precarious position. If they acknowledged Jesus, their pride in their position would take a hit. They would have to admit that they had not listened to the prophets, had not cared for what God wanted from them. In fact, they would have to let go of everything in order to follow this "son" who didn't fit their idea of a Messiah.

Jesus never wanted the Pharisees to be lost. He never wanted to have to bring punishment on Israel, but they were ignoring every message that God sent them. He simply wanted to get their attention, to get them to think of what it might be like if the tenants killed the son. And they got it. They understood that he was speaking about them and still, they wanted to kill him.

What about you? Do you want to live a life apart from God? Jesus wanted to make things clear. What is he trying to say to you through this parable?

We are such frail beings. We want what we want. But think about it this way. What is it that you want that might be getting in the way of truly following Jesus? What things? What positions? What renown? Is it worth it to pursue the earthly things, when the God of heaven wants to give you the best thing – Jesus himself?

Journal your thoughts:

_____

_____

_____

_____

_____

_____

_____

_____

_____

_____

_____

_____

_____

_____

_____

_____

_____

Two Commandments
Mark 12:18-44

These verses speak of the struggles people were having with various teachings. Was there a resurrection of the body? What was the most important commandment? How much should I give? How could Jesus be David's "son"? Who was right about all these things?

It is true in our day as well. We have so many denominations squabbling about who is right. We have schisms and church splits. We have broken relationships that refuse to be mended. And God is not pleased. I don't know which group you belong to or what your statement of beliefs is but there are some basics that we need to acknowledge so that we can come together in Christ.

Jesus responds to the Sadducees, the teachers and those that refused to listen by stating clearly what was important. Here is our starting place. "Hear, O Israel, the Lord our God, the Lord is one. Love the Lord your God with all your heart and with all your soul and with all your mind and with all your strength.' The second is this: 'Love your neighbor as yourself'." Jesus was saying very clearly that all their questioning, all their bickering was irrelevant. What mattered were these two interconnected statements that were more important than burnt offerings.

Do you hear it. God does not want offerings that mean nothing to us. He wants us to love. He doesn't want a little of our lives (the gifts that require little of us) but all of ourselves (the widow's offering). Jesus says we are focused on the wrong things – again. It's not about our pet theological point or our traditions. It IS about living like Jesus did, honoring God with his every breath and loving those who were being ignored because their leaders were "walking around in flowing robes" hoping to be seen.

Everyone was missing the point! Jesus was both David's son (human) and David's Lord (God). He was here to teach us to make the main point the main point. It was time to drop all the pretenses and get on with living for God.

Now don't get me wrong, I love a good theological discussion. I can get so caught up in it that I too miss the point of my relationship with God and others. Before all things, we are told to seek God's kingdom and that means living out the Great Commandments. So, go on. Spend some deep time with God and then go out and spread the good news by loving those around you.

Journal your thoughts:

_____

_____

_____

_____

_____

_____

_____

_____

_____

_____

_____

_____

_____

_____

_____

_____

End Times
Mark 13:1-37

Many people are fascinated by end-times theology. They scour the prophecies in hope of getting a clear picture of when and how it will happen. We have books and films about it. The Left Behind series is one of many that take a particular point of view and create stories around it. Various theories have set groups apart, again bringing discord rather than unity to the body.

Eschatology – the study of the end times – offers three major possibilities for the return of Christ. Pre-millennialism suggests that Christ will return and then there will be a period of time on earth where he reigns. Post-millennialism says that Christ's return will happen following a millennial period of the Kingdom. Amillennialism says that there will not be an earthly literal reign of Jesus.

Here Jesus says we are to watch for signs, but at the same time, we are not to jump to conclusions. He shares two prophecies, just as the prophets of old did. The first is an imminent disaster, the destruction of Jerusalem. The second is a future event, Christ's return. Each of these will be accompanied by signs and forewarnings.

As Jesus sits with his disciples on the Mount of Olives, he is preparing them for what is to come. He offers information and warnings so that they can be prepared for it all. Sitting there, they must have had a lot of fear and concern. "How will we be able to handle this?" "What do we tell people?" And especially, "When will you come back?"

If only it was clear. If only he had said the year. But it was not to be so and so we wait.

What are we to do while we wait? Jesus uses a number of warnings and exhortations. First, don't be deceived. Many would come claiming to be him, but his believers needed to be discerning, not falling for their smooth talk. Second, there will be personal danger. For all our talk about how Jesus makes our lives better (and he does), we need to recognize that staying true to the end is not easy. We will be persecuted, maybe even killed for our faith. Many are dying even now around the world for the cause of Christ. Third, we will have to speak up, but don't worry, the Holy Spirit will give us the words.

Jesus ends this section with the parable of the homeowner. The message is clear. Be alert! Be on guard! Don't be spiritually lazy, because the time will come when you least expect it. This is not a threat but a reality. The end will come, and we must maintain our faith though we don't see any signs.

Stand firm! Put on the armor! Be ready! Our King is coming!

Journal your thoughts:

_____

_____

_____

_____

_____

_____

_____

_____

_____

_____

_____

_____

_____

_____

_____

_____

_____

Sacrifice
Mark 14:1-3

Whether your tradition does anything with Lent or not, it is a great time to take stock in your walk with Jesus, to think about things that hinder it and to shed them, at least for a time, in order that you might grow closer to God.

Mary washes Jesus' feet with an enormous sacrifice. What do you make of this when you read it? Was Judas right? Sometimes a sacrifice looks crazy, doesn't it? We give what we can't afford out of love and people think we are nuts. Yet, Mary's gift was all about the one she loved, her Savior and Friend. Are you willing to sacrifice something for him? What might it be?

In the Upper Room, Jesus takes the Passover meal and connects it to all his teachings about himself. "This is my body, this is my blood." For the most part, we celebrate communion as a separate event. Whether it is every week, once a month or once a year, we do it together as a symbol of our faith. Here, Jesus is sharing the Passover with his closest friends. It is a special occasion, a time set apart for them to remember and be thankful. The slow and steady progression of his ministry to the cross stops for a moment to remember the works of God.

Passover is both serious and joyful. It is a time of sacrifice (which is why Jesus died during it) and a time of rejoicing for the salvation of Israel from Egypt. Jesus finally puts his stake in the ground. He is the Passover Lamb, the final sacrifice. His body, his blood, shed for us for the forgiveness of sins. How seriously we should take this, yet how joyfully.

Jesus told the disciples they would all fall away for a time. Maybe that's where you are. You've had a tough time and you've given up. Rise up and come back because Jesus is worth the sacrifice.

Journal your thoughts:

_____

_____

_____

_____

_____

_____

_____

_____

_____

_____

_____

_____

_____

_____

_____

_____

_____

God's Will
Mark 14:32-52

Jesus had been telling the disciples all along that he had come to do the Father's will. As he entered the garden, this must have been the foremost thought in his mind: "I am here to do His will." And yet, his prayer reminds us that he was not just God but also man, fully capable of human emotions and anxieties. He was aware of his path but asked for a different choice.

He must have hidden those feelings well, because the disciples were able to fall asleep, unaware of the turmoil in their friend. They still couldn't fully grasp his plan; couldn't understand why he was worried that they would fall away when the hard times came. They still weren't sure that someone would betray him. So, they waited and slept.

In a way, we have become like the disciples, unable to stay the course, asleep at our post. Our world is a mess, our children are killing each other and yet we act like nothing is happening. How can we sit idle while the world is dying? The disciples had fallen into a comfortable routine and, though they were warned, they continued.

And then it happened. Judas really did betray Jesus. The disciples really did scatter and fall away. Jesus really did get arrested. What does it take for us to see that God knows and sees and wants us to stand up for right and hope in a hopeless world? What will it take to stop the shootings and the hatred, the bitter words and the vicious talk?

Jesus came for this moment and every moment. He came to stand in the gap between humanity and God. And even though he had a moment where he wished there was another way, he did the Father's will.

In a world of turmoil, what is the Father asking of you? Can you say, "Your will be done?" Will you stand with Jesus for the healing of our land, our planet? There is only one side to be on and that's God's.

Journal your thoughts:

_____

_____

_____

_____

_____

_____

_____

_____

_____

_____

_____

_____

_____

_____

_____

Cue the Rooster
Mark 14:53-72

Have you ever lived near a rooster? I have. He delighted in crowing at four in the morning. Now, I'm an early riser, but four? No thank you. Here is Peter, waiting all night for word of what has happened to Jesus, and the rooster crows – on cue. "I don't know him." (Cue the rooster). Three times, just like Jesus told him it would.

The words for Peter's reaction to that sound are "broke down and wept." My word would be devastation. All the disciples must have felt some sense of failure, some recognition of their great cowardice, but for Peter, the rock, it must have been 100 times worse. Inside the building, Jesus is being flogged and spat upon, but outside Peter is protecting his own reputation. Do you see the contrast?

"Are you the Messiah?" "I am."

"Weren't you with him?" "I was not."

Truth and lie together in one place. And so it is for all of us. We want to be the strong disciple, the one who vows that they will never deny him, but in fact we are just as likely as Peter to fail, to fall away when things get tough.

And this is why Jesus came, why he taught, why he endured the cross, because we needed someone to save us from ourselves. Whatever your sin, whatever your struggle, Jesus came for you just as he came for Peter. In John 21, Jesus settles the score for him.

"Peter, do you love me?" And Peter's honest answer is "Yes, Lord, I'm working on it." And that's all he asks.

The rooster is up with the sun, and the good news is that there is redemption for our sin, for the many ways that we deny knowing Jesus. "_____ (your name), do you love me?" I hope your answer is yes.

Journal your thoughts:

_____

_____

_____

_____

_____

_____

_____

_____

_____

_____

_____

_____

_____

_____

_____

_____

_____

Crucify Him
Mark 15:1-20

"Crucify him!" It probably started as a few well-placed voices in the crowd. Many who were there weren't really on any side, but the voices began to swell. In essence, it became a mob, bursting into shouts of hatred, stirred by the leaders of the Jews. One voice, then a few, then many. They were too loud. They drowned out those who were shouting for Jesus. It hurts just to think about it.

And Jesus stood there. The day before, he had told God he was ready to do His will. How hard it must have been for his human heart and mind to comprehend such hatred, such venom toward him. Sure, he had made the leaders angry, called them out, but this? And yet, he just stood there.

Finally, Pilate had to make a choice. While Mark doesn't mention it, Matthew states that he washed his hands, claiming no fault in the decision. Once that was done, Pilate walked away, leaving Jesus in the hands of the soldiers. Roman soldiers were notoriously brutal, and they didn't hold back as they prepared Jesus for crucifixion. The crown of thorns pressed down hard on his head. The robe of purple, signifying kingship. The mocking, beating, spitting. They had no stake in the quarrel between Jesus and the Jews. They had no reason to be harsh in their actions. It was all funny to them. And Jesus stood there and took it.

Why? Did he know that this story would be told for thousands of years? Did he know that every person that heard it would wonder at him? Why didn't he fight? Why didn't he defend himself? Why?

There are people still today who would do the same, who would mock and laugh at him, at us, for believing in him. He stood there to acknowledge how broken our world was and is. He stood there to tell us that it isn't so much about fighting back as it is about staying the course. He stood there to make it clear that his message was one of peace and patience and love. He stood there for you and for me and for those who would mock him.

So today, as you go about your life, think about what God might want you to do. How might he want you to stand firm, to stay the course? How might he want you to see the truth that you have been avoiding, that Jesus died because he loved all of us, even the ones who shouted "crucify?" What next step might God be asking you to take to help bring in his Kingdom?

Behold, Jesus. King of kings and Lord of lords! He stood there for you.

Journal your thoughts:

_____

_____

_____

_____

_____

_____

_____

_____

_____

_____

_____

_____

_____

_____

_____

All for You
Mark 15:21-47

It seems so surreal. He performed so many miracles for others, why wouldn't he save himself? But that's the message, isn't it. It's not about Jesus for Jesus' sake. It's about how much he loves us, all of us, and in one selfless act, he did the unimaginable. He died for us.

Mark continues his very concise telling of the story. There are many parts that aren't here: the words to the thief on the cross, the other things Jesus said. Yet, the bare facts tell us so much. They tell us of more mocking and harassment. They tell us of his agony. They tell us that there were some who stood near in support and some who stood near to gloat. They tell us about the six hours of pain, humiliation and struggle that Jesus endured for us.

I guess I need to read this more often because it can become just a story in my head. It can become a sideline to the miracles and the story that follows. But I need to pause here, to witness the most important event in history and set it in its rightful place – first and foremost.

For what has Jesus done during his Passion? He has taken the abuse that I deserve and carried my cross to the hill of pain. Just as I do, he struggled to breathe and wondered if the Father would save him. He felt abandoned and hopeless so that I could be adopted and hopeful. Jesus gave his life for his friends, you and me, so that we could be with him and live for him.

What is your struggle? Jesus gets it. What is your pain? Jesus feels it. What makes you feel hopeless? Jesus has been there, and he is there with you.

Don't rush past this passage. Spend time here, at the cross with Jesus. Meditate on his agony, mental, emotional, physical and spiritual. Recognize the enormity of what he did and why he did it.

What a wonderful Savior!

Journal your thoughts:

_____

_____

_____

_____

_____

_____

_____

_____

_____

_____

_____

_____

_____

_____

_____

_____

The
Journey
Continues

Risen Indeed
Mark 16:1-20

He is risen!

The women get up early on Sunday morning, prepared to care for Jesus' body. They head to the tomb, wondering who will move the stone for them so that they can do what the women always did. As they look ahead, they see that the stone is already moved. Did someone come ahead of them? Did the disciples already show up?

A "young man" was waiting there, all dressed in white. In the other gospels, he is referred to as an angel and his words here would indicate that. Every encounter with an angel begins with words like "do not be alarmed" or terrified or afraid. He then gives them instructions to go and tell the disciples (and Peter) that Jesus has risen.

Bewildered, the women leave and for a time they say nothing. We know from the other gospels that it wasn't long before they did go to the disciples, but Mark does not tell us that.

The book of Mark ends abruptly at verse 8. (The early manuscripts do not contain verses 9-20.) Why would Mark stop before the entire story was told? Why would he leave his readers hanging? Remember that Mark had an agenda to write a clear concise picture of the events.

At some point in time, someone wrote the conclusion that is included. The language and style are very different from Mark's. It also has some confusing messages about snakes and poison. It is assumed that these refer to punishments used on the disciples for preaching the Gospel and that the Lord saved them from the harmful effects. At any rate, these verses were added to the text so that those who read it would know "the rest of the story."

The women, confused and scared, were left to carry the message. Jesus promised to meet the disciples in Galilee. We know they went. We know that he gave them the Great Commission. We know that their lives changed, their faith was strengthened and that they stopped being afraid. But that morning, even with hope in their hearts, they were still scared.

In the end, what matters is that Jesus had risen and appeared to the women and the disciples. As the song says, "Because he lives, all fear is gone."

Journal your thoughts:

_____

_____

_____

_____

_____

_____

_____

_____

_____

_____

_____

_____

_____

_____

_____

_____

_____

_____

Information on the Gospel of Mark

The Gospel of Mark is attributed it to John Mark, who traveled with Peter. Whether Mark actually wrote the book or not is questioned by scholars; we can only wonder who else might have written it. What we do know is that it was written in Greek between 66-70 CE.

This gospel was originally thought to have been the second one written, hence its place in our Bibles. But studies have now placed it as the first. It was probably written to the Gentiles to counter some misconceptions about how Jesus fit in with the message of the Old Testament. Mark certainly had a theological agenda, desiring to teach how Jesus saw the Kingdom of God and his part in it.

As part of the "synoptic" gospels, Mark contains many of the events and parables found in Luke and Matthew. He chose the ones he used to further his teachings of theology. His gospel contains no genealogy, or early record of Jesus, jumping in at his baptism and calling of the disciples. Mark is a concise writer, a "just the facts" kind of guy, who wants his message to be clear and unclouded.

The gospel ends rather abruptly with the women running from the tomb. A later addition to the text shares the message from Jesus to take the gospel to the world. This addition is included in our Bibles today but was probably written much later and added early in the second century.

In all, this Gospel gives a clear recitation of Jesus ministry and message. I pray that you will take what you have read and share the story of Jesus with those who cross your path.

Printed in the United States
By Bookmasters